I0454594

Copyright © 2024 Steph Wynne
Published by Skinny Books Publishing
Cover design: Steph Wynne

For more information:

Skinny Books Publishing
PO BOX 34652
Los Angeles, CA 90034

www.skinnybookspublishing.com

ISBN# 9798871383933

# Welcome

In California, businesses are subject to several types of taxes, each depending on the nature and structure of the business.

Here's an overview of common business taxes in California:

**California Corporate Tax:** Most businesses are charged a California corporate tax. This is applicable depending on the type of business entity they operate. Additionally, income that passes through a business is also subject to the California state income tax.

**California Alternative Minimum Tax (AMT):** Businesses may also be subject to the California AMT. This is particularly relevant for businesses that may not owe substantial regular corporate taxes due to deductions and credits.

**California Franchise Tax:** This tax is applicable to different types of business entities, including C corporations, S corporations, and Limited Liability Companies (LLCs).

C corporations pay a franchise tax of a flat rate of 8.84%, which applies to those that report net taxable income. In the absence of a profit, a flat AMT of 6.65% is levied. S corporations are generally taxed at 1.5% of their net income or a minimum franchise tax of $800, whichever is larger. LLCs are required to pay a minimum of $800 in franchise taxes, although the exact amount varies based on the LLC's net income.

**Sales Taxes:** Businesses in California are also subject to sales taxes. This applies to businesses that sell goods or certain services. The sales tax rate varies depending on the location within California, as local jurisdictions may add to the state sales tax rate.

**Employment Taxes:** For businesses with employees, there are various employment taxes that must be considered. These include taxes like payroll taxes, unemployment insurance taxes, and disability insurance.

It's important to note that the exact tax liabilities can vary greatly depending on the specific circumstances of a business, including its legal structure and the nature of its operations.

Business owners are advised to consult with a tax professional to understand their specific tax obligations and ensure compliance with California tax laws.

# Disclaimer

The Ultimate Tax & Compliance Cheat Sheet offers general information and does not constitute legal, accounting, or professional advice. While we strive for accuracy, tax laws change and may vary by circumstance.

This handbook is not a replacement for professional guidance. Please consult experts for specific matters before decisions. We are not liable for any losses resulting from information use.

Verify information with tax agencies and consult official sources for current guidance.

# Table of Contents

# Introduction

Welcome to "The Ultimate Tax & Compliance Cheat Sheet," your indispensable guide to navigating the complexities of business taxes in California.

Whether you're a seasoned entrepreneur or just starting out, this cheat sheet is designed to simplify the often daunting world of business taxation and compliance.

In California's dynamic business environment, understanding your tax obligations is crucial. Our cheat sheet demystifies common taxes like the California Corporate Tax, the California Franchise Tax, Employment Tax, and more.

We delve into the specifics of tax rates that corporations and LLCs encounter, along with the varying franchise tax rates based on their net income.

Additionally, we address the nuances of sales and employment taxes, ensuring you have a complete picture of your potential liabilities.

But it's not just about tax rates and forms. This guide is your roadmap to hassle-free business taxes, providing essential insights into tax rates, due dates, and compliance requirements across different business structures. From payroll due dates to local levies, and from Secretary of State filings to state income tax considerations, we've got you covered.

As a business owner, staying ahead of your tax obligations is key to success. However, remember that tax laws are ever-evolving, and this guide should be used as a starting point. For personalized advice, always consult with a tax professional.

Embark on your journey to tax mastery with "The Ultimate Tax & Compliance Cheat Sheet." Let's simplify taxes, one step at a time.

# How to Use This Cheat Sheet

☐ Check off each item that applies to your business

☐ Write the name of the agency if it is not included

☐ Make sure that you review your cheat sheet check every three months or if not you, have your bookkeeper or office manager.

Make sure all your forms and payments are up to date.

# BUSINESS TAXES

*Required by all income business types*

**Entity:** IRS.gov
**Tax Type:** Federal
**Annual Due Date:** April 15th
*(extensions are usually granted to October 15th)*

**Tax Forms:** *Check which entity applies to you*

- ☐ Form 1120 - Corporation
- ☐ Form 1120S - S. Corporation *Due March 15th*
- ☐ Form 1065 - Partnership
- ☐ Form 1040/Schedule C - Sole Proprietor
- ☐ Estimated taxes are due qtrly

---

**Entity:** Franchise Tax Board - ftb.ca.gov
**Tax Type:** State of California
**Annual Due Date:** April 15th
*(extensions are automatic to October 15th, however $800 fee is still  due)*

**Tax Forms:** *Check which entity applies to you*

- ☐ Form 100 *(Corporations)*
- ☐ Form 100-S *(S. Corporations)*
- ☐ Form 568 *(LLC)*
- ☐ *Form 565 (LLP)*
- ☐ *Form 540 (Sole Proprietor) (No $800 fee sole proprietors)*
- ☐ Estimated taxes are due qtrly

**Entity:** County of Assessor - assessor.lacounty.gov
**Tax Type:** Property
**Annual Due Date:** April 1st

☐ Form 571 L - *(Business property ie tax desks, computers etc.)*

---

**Entity:** Office of Finance - Finance.lacity.gov
**Tax Type:** Local City *(income inside or outside of Los Angeles)*
**Annual Due Date:** February 28th

☐ Form ID 64

---

**Entity:** CDTFA.gov
*California Department of Tax and Fee Administration*
**Tax Type:** Sales Tax *(income inside or outside of Los Angeles)*
**Annual Due Date:** Quarterly

☐ Rates

---

**Entity:** Secretary of State - Sos.ca.gov
**Type:** Statement of Income *(Entities only ie LLC, LLP, Corps.)*
**Due Every 2 years:** January 1st

☐ Form SI-100

*Does not apply to sole proprietors*

---

**FICTITIOUS BUSINESS NAME** - lavote.gov
☐ DBA - Renewal every 5 years

# EMPLOYEE PAYROLL TAXES

*(If no employees skip this section)*

**Entity:** IRS.gov
**Tax Type:** Federal
**Annual Due Date:** December 31st

☐ **Form W2** *Due to employees annually*

The W-2 form is a crucial tax document that provides a comprehensive overview of an employee's earnings and tax withholdings for a specific calendar year.

irs.gov/pub/irs-pdf/fw2.pdf

---

**Entity:** IRS.gov
**Tax Type:** Federal
**Annual Due Date:** December 31st

☐ **Form W3** *Filed annually by employer*

The W-3 form is a transmittal form used to report and summarize the information contained in the W-2 forms. Employers use the W-3 to provide an overview of their employees' wage and salary details, along with tax withholdings, to the Social Security Administration (SSA).

irs.gov/pub/irs-prior/fw3--2023.pdf

**Entity:** IRS.gov
**Tax Type:** Federal
**Due Date:** Quarterly

☐ **Form 941** *(due quarterly or annually)*

**Form 941** is a quarterly return that focuses on reporting income tax, Social Security tax, and Medicare tax withheld from employees' paychecks, as well as employer contributions to Social Security and Medicare.

https://www.irs.gov/pub/irs-pdf/f941.pdf

---

**Entity:** IRS.gov
**Tax Type:** Federal
**Annual Due Date:** January 31st

☐ **Form 940** *(due annually)*

**Form 940**, on the other hand, is an annual return specifically for reporting and paying federal unemployment taxes (FUTA) and is filed once a year. Both forms are essential for employers to fulfill their payroll tax obligations and maintain compliance with federal tax regulations.

https://www.irs.gov/pub/irs-pdf/f940.pdf

**Entity:** EDD.ca.gov
(Employment Development Department | California)
**Tax Type:** State of California
**Due Date:** Quarterly

☐ DE-9 *(due quarterly)*

**DE-9 form**, also known as the Quarterly Contribution Return and Report of Wages, is a quarterly report required by the California Employment Development Department (EDD).

Employers use this form to report their employees' wage and employment information, including taxable wages and contributions to unemployment insurance, disability insurance, and employment training taxes.

---

**Entity:** EDD.ca.gov
(Employment Development Department | California)
**Tax Type:** State of California
**Due Date:** Quarterly

☐ DE-9C (due quarterly)

**DE-9C** form, often referred to as the Quarterly Contribution Return and Report of Wages (Continuation), is a supplementary form that accompanies the DE-9. It provides additional details on employee wage and tax information, broken down by individual employees.

# SMALL BUSINESS AND SELF EMPLOYED

**Entity:** IRS.gov
**Tax Type:** Federal
**Annual Due Date:** January 31st

☐ W-9 *(filled out by contractor kept on file by business)*

☐ 1099 K, 1099 MISC and 1099 NEC
*(Due to SBASE January 31st)*

## 1. FORM 1099-K *(Payment Card and 3rd Party Network Transactions)*

The 1099-K form is used to report payment transactions made through payment card transactions (like credit cards) and third-party payment networks (like PayPal).

## 2. FORM 1099-NEC *(Nonemployee Compensation)*

The 1099-NEC form is specifically used to report payments made to non-employees, such as independent contractors, freelancers, or other service providers.

## 3. FORM 1099-MISC *(Miscellaneous Income)*

The 1099-MISC form is used for various types of income that don't fit into other 1099 categories. It was previously used for reporting nonemployee compensation before the introduction of 1099-NEC.

# EMPLOYMENT TAX RATES

*(If no employees skip this section)*

**FEDERAL** Payroll Tax Rates for 2024 are:

☐ Social Security tax rate: 6.2% for the employee plus 6.2% for the employer.

☐ Medicare tax rate: 1.45% for the employee plus 1.45% for the employer.

☐ Additional Medicare: 0.9% for the employee when wages exceed $200,000 in a year.

## STATE

☐ SDI withholding rate for 2024 is 1.1 percent.

*Effective January 1, 2024, Senate Bill 951 removes the taxable wage limit and maximum withholdings for each employee subject to SDI contributions. Thus no limit on SDI taxable wages.*

☐ Unemployment Insurance Tax (UI) 1.5 to 6.2%

☐ Employment Training Tax (ETT) 0.1%

# BUSINESS TAX RATES

California Corporate income tax rate 2024 - **8.84**

Since passing the Tax Cuts and Jobs Act of 2017, the Federal Corporate Tax Rate has been 21%.

- ☐ Corporation (C Corp): 21% Flat Rate

- ☐ S. Corporations: 10%–37% (K-1)*

- ☐ Partnerships: 10%–37% (K-1)*

- ☐ Limited liability corporations (LLCs): 10%–37% (Schedule C)

- ☐ Sole proprietorships: 10%–37% (Schedule C)

*Past thru to 1040 (profit or loss goes on K-1)*

# WORKERS COMPENSATION

☐ Due Monthly
☐ Due Annually

**Workers' compensation** in California is a vital safety net for employees, ensuring they receive necessary medical care and financial support in the event of workplace injuries or illnesses. Employers are legally obligated to provide this coverage to protect their workers and themselves from costly legal actions.

## 401k CONTRIBUTIONS

☐ Every paycheck

# TAX DUE DATES BY MONTH

*Most tax forms and payments can be filed online.

## January
- 1099-NEC, 1099-MISC., and 1099-K due to contractors, small businesses, self employed *(due 31st)*

## February
- 1099's - Business to IRS *(due 28th)*
- Office of Finance *(due 28th)*

## March
- IRS 941 *(due qtrly)* Payment due April 30th
- EDD DE9/DE9C *(due qtrly)*
- S. Corporation *(due 15th)*
- Sales Taxes *(due qtrly)*

## April
- IRS Federal - *(due 15th)*
  *Corporations, LLC's, LLP, Sole proprietors*
- Franchise Tax Board - *(due on 15th)*
  ($800 franchise fee is also due)

## June
- 941 *(due qtrly)* Payment due July 31st
- DE9/DE9C *(due qtrly 30th)*
- Sales taxes *(due qtrly)*

## July
- County of Los Angeles Property Tax *(due 31st)*

## October
- Federal extensions 15th
- State is usually automatic 15th

## December
- 941 4th Quarter *(due qtrly)*, (Payment due January 31st of following year)
- DE9/DE9C (due qtrly)
- W2's to employees *(1st week of January)*
- 1099's to contractors *(1st week in January)*

# CASE STUDY - A True Story

## Joe's Transformation: From Tax Chaos to Tax Organization and Compliance

In Sun Valley, California there was a business owner named Joe. Joe owned a small but thriving hardware store, known for its friendly service and an impressive array of tools.

But behind the scenes, Joe struggled with a significant challenge: managing his business's taxes and payroll taxes. Joe, a determined do-it-yourselfer, handled all his payroll and business tax responsibilities.

However, his desk was a mountain of forms and calendars, and despite his best efforts, he always seemed to miss crucial due dates. Late fees accumulated, and the stress began to weigh heavily on him. He knew something had to change.

One day, Joe stumbled upon "The Ultimate Tax & Compliance Cheat Sheet" while browsing online. Intrigued by the promise of a simpler way to manage his tax obligations, he decided to give it a try.

The cheat sheet was a revelation for Joe. It was like having a personal tax assistant by his side.

The guide clearly listed all the tax forms he needed, along with their due dates and online links with detailed instructions on how to file them. It even included information on payroll taxes for both federal and state levels, which was a game-changer for him.

With the cheat sheet, Joe finally had a clear roadmap. He started planning ahead, using the cheat sheet to mark important dates on his calendar and set reminders.

The once-daunting task of sorting through various tax forms became manageable. He was no longer sifting through piles of paper to find the right form or scrambling at the last minute to meet deadlines.

The real test came at the end of the quarter. For the first time in years, Joe filed all his tax forms on time. He even managed to submit his employees' payroll without any hiccups. The sense of accomplishment he felt was immense.

Joe's newfound confidence in handling his business's financial obligations had a ripple effect. He was more relaxed, his focus on customer service improved, and he even found time to brainstorm new ideas for his store.

His employees noticed the change too; the atmosphere at work became more positive and energetic. "The Ultimate Tax & Compliance Cheat Sheet" didn't just help Joe stay on top of his tax obligations; it transformed the way he ran his business.

Joe realized that sometimes, seeking help – even in the form of a cheat sheet – wasn't a sign of weakness but a step towards greater efficiency and success.

From that day on, Joe's store wasn't just known for its tools and friendly service but also as a testament to the power of staying organized and informed.

Joe became an advocate for the cheat sheet, often sharing his story with fellow business owners, inspiring them to take control of their tax obligations.

And so, Joe continued his journey, no longer a stressed business owner but a savvy, well-prepared entrepreneur, all thanks to a simple yet powerful tool that turned his tax chaos into an organizational and understanding triumph.

This cheat sheet not only streamlined his tax filing process but also enhanced his comprehension of the intricacies of business taxation.

Joe's new found grasp of deadlines, forms, and rates empowered him to make more informed financial decisions for his business.

No longer in the shadows of confusion and last-minute rushes, he operated with a clarity that brought peace of mind and a newfound sense of control over his business's financial health.

The cheat sheet, once a mere guide, had become an integral part of Joe's business toolkit, a symbol of his growth from a reactive business owner to a proactive, strategic thinker!

This story is Joe's testimony! Thank you Joe!

# GLOSSARY

## Sole Proprietorship:

- **Structure:** An unincorporated business owned and run by one individual with no distinction between the business and the owner.
- **Liability:** The owner is personally liable for all debts and obligations of the business.
- **Taxes:** Profits or losses are reported on the owner's personal income tax returns; there is no separate business tax return.

## Limited Liability Company (LLC):

- **Structure:** A hybrid entity combining characteristics of both a corporation and a partnership or sole proprietorship.
- **Liability:** Offers limited liability protection to its owners (known as members), meaning personal assets are generally protected from business debts.
- **Taxes:** Can choose to be taxed as a sole proprietor, partnership, S corporation, or C corporation, offering flexibility.

## Limited Liability Partnership (LLP):

- **Structure:** A partnership in which some or all partners have limited liabilities, protecting them from the debts of the partnership.
- **Liability:** Each partner is protected from debts against the partnership arising from professional malpractice lawsuits against another partner.
- **Taxes:** Income is passed through to partners and reported on their personal tax returns.

## S Corporation (S Corp):

- **Structure:** A special type of corporation created through an IRS tax election which allows profits, and some losses, to be passed directly to owners' personal income without being subject to corporate tax rates.
- **Liability:** Offers limited liability protection to its shareholders.
- **Taxes:** Avoids double taxation typically incurred by a C corporation but is subject to certain qualifications.

## Corporation (C Corp):

- **Structure:** A legal entity separate from its owners (shareholders), offering the strongest protection from personal liability.

- **Liability:** Shareholders are typically not personally responsible for business debts and liabilities.
- **Taxes:** Subject to corporate income tax; profits distributed as dividends are taxed at the shareholder's personal tax rate, leading to double taxation.

**1099-K** *(Payment Card and Third Party Network Transactions)*

- **Purpose:** The 1099-K form is used to report payment transactions made through payment card transactions (like credit cards) and third-party payment networks (like PayPal).
- **Who Receives It:** It is typically issued to merchants or other entities who accept payment card transactions, or to those who receive payments through third-party networks, if the payments exceed a certain threshold.
- **What It Reports:** The form reports the gross amount of all reportable transactions within a calendar year. It includes the total number of transactions, but does not take into account returns, refunds, or any other expenses.

**1099-NEC** *(Nonemployee Compensation)*

- **Purpose:** The 1099-NEC form is specifically used to report payments made to non-employees, such as independent contractors, freelancers, or other service providers.

**Who Receives It:** It is typically sent to individuals or entities that have received at least $600 during the year in compensation for services provided to a business that is not their employer.

- **What It Reports:** This form reports the total amount of nonemployee compensation, covering fees, commissions, prizes, and other forms of payment for services rendered by someone who is not an employee.

## 1099-MISC *(Miscellaneous Income)*

- **Purpose:** The 1099-MISC form is used for various types of income that don't fit into other 1099 categories. It was previously used for reporting nonemployee compensation before the introduction of 1099-NEC.

- **Who Receives It:** This form is issued to individuals or entities who have received certain types of income, such as rent, royalties, awards, medical and health care payments, or other miscellaneous income.

- **What It Reports:** The form reports various types of income such as rent, royalties, awards, and other types of income not covered by other 1099 forms.

## Business Property Tax

**What's Taxed:** Business property taxes in counties like Los Angeles often apply to tangible property used in a business. This includes items like computers, furniture, equipment, and machinery.

**Tax Basis:** The tax is usually based on the assessed value of the property. This value may be determined annually and can be based on the original purchase price and depreciation.

**Filing Requirements:** Business owners are generally required to file a property statement each year, declaring all the taxable property they own. This statement helps the assessor determine the property's value.

**Tax Rates:** The tax rate can vary but is often a percentage of the assessed value. This rate is typically set by the local county tax authorities.

**Due Dates and Penalties:** There are specific deadlines for filing property tax statements and for paying the taxes due. Late filings or payments can result in penalties.

For the most accurate and detailed information, it's recommended to consult the Los Angeles County Assessor's Office or a local tax professional.
They can provide the specific rates, forms, and due dates applicable to businesses in Los Angeles County.

**Sales taxes** – Businesses in California are also subject to sales taxes. This applies to businesses that sell products or certain services.

The sales tax rate varies depending on the cities within California.

**Income taxes** – Income taxes are levied on individuals and businesses by local governments.